COOL TO BE KIND

What's the coolest thing you can think of?

Being a top gamer?

Having a YouTube channel?

Being in a dance crew?

Scoring the winning goal in the FA Cup?

What about having a superpower?

What does it mean to be cool?

Does it mean being...

... admired?

... liked?

... looked up to?

... positive?

... confident?

... someone that other people want to be with, want to know, want to hang out with?

... someone you want to be like when you grow up?

... someone you dream about meeting?

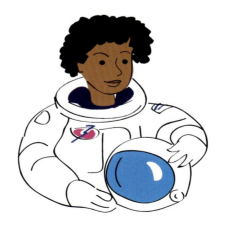

COOL TO BE KIND

This illustrated storybook introduces Coco, Otto, Ollie and Ling as they negotiate the sometimes tricky world of friendships and relationships, observing the unkindness of some and using their superpower – kindness – to change the lives of others. Explore with them what it means to be unkind, why that choice is sometimes made and how usually there is another choice – to be kind.

This storybook will:

• Help facilitate discussions with children about values, morals and empathy

• Support children to see that kindness can be a cool choice to make

• Help you to introduce children to the notion that kindness and unkindness are choices

This storybook is available to purchase as part of a two-component set, *Negotiating the World of Friendships and Relationships: A 'Cool to be Kind' Storybook and Practical Resource*. It can be used by teachers and support staff to teach and promote kindness to children at primary age and beyond.

Liz Bates is an independent education consultant. She supports both primary and secondary schools in all aspects of Emotional Health and Wellbeing, including whole school approaches, training staff and delivering talks to parents. Liz is a Protective Behaviours Trainer, a Wellbeing Award Advisor for Optimus and a Schools Engagement Trainer for The Anna Freud Centre.

Cool to be Kind

How to Negotiate the World of Friendships and Relationships

Liz Bates

Illustrated by Nigel Dodds

Routledge
Taylor & Francis Group
LONDON AND NEW YORK

First published 2021
by Routledge
2 Park Square, Milton Park, Abingdon, Oxon OX14 4RN

and by Routledge
52 Vanderbilt Avenue, New York, NY 10017

Routledge is an imprint of the Taylor & Francis Group, an informa business

British Library Cataloguing-in-Publication Data
A catalogue record for this book is available from the British Library

Library of Congress Cataloging-in-Publication Data
Names: Bates, Liz, author. | Dodds, Nigel (Archaeological illustrator), illustrator.
Title: Cool to be kind: how to negotiate the world of friendships and relationships/Liz Bates; illustrated by Nigel Dodds.
Description: Abingdon, Oxon; New York, NY: Routledge, 2021. |
Summary: Coco, Otto, Ollie, and Ling negotiate the sometimes tricky world of friendships and relationships, observing the unkindness of some and using kindness to change the lives of others.
Identifiers: LCCN 2020034624 (print) | LCCN 2020034625 (ebook) |
ISBN 9780367679996 (pbk) | ISBN 9781003133759 (ebk)
Subjects: CYAC: Kindness–Fiction. | Friendship–Fiction. |
Interpersonal relations–Fiction.
Classification: LCC PZ7.1.B37725 Co 2021 (print) |
LCC PZ7.1.B37725 (ebook) | DDC [Fic]–dc23
LC record available at https://lccn.loc.gov/2020034624
LC ebook record available at https://lccn.loc.gov/2020034625

ISBN: 978-0-367-67999-6 (pbk)
ISBN: 978-1-003-13375-9 (ebk)

Typeset in Calibri
by Newgen Publishing UK

Does some of that sound tough to do?

So if, at the moment, you're not in a dance crew, or likely to be picked for the FA Cup squad, what can you do?

Well, there is another way to be cool.

It's something you can do.

It's something everyone can do.

It's a superpower that everyone can have.

Meet Coco, Otto, Ollie and Ling.

They all have a superpower. It's not the strength to bend iron bars, or the ability to fly. They can't turn themselves into blocks of ice or see through walls.

But their superpower still helps other people.

In fact, it can help everyone, all of the time.

Hi Coco.

Coco loves football and she plays in the school football team.

The team made it to the final and played a team from another school.

On the morning of the final the usual goalie was sick, so Kez volunteered to be substitute.

The other team scored three goals and Coco's team lost.

After the match Coco could hear some of the team talking about Kez.

They were making fun of Kez, calling him names because he let in three goals.

Someone shouted "he's useless, we don't want him on the team".

Coco thought how unfair everyone was being. She thought that being substitute goalie was really tough.

Coco knew it was time for her superpower.
KINDNESS

Coco tells Kez how brave it is to be goalie sub. No-one else volunteered. If they hadn't had a goalie, the team would have been disqualified.

So Kez enabled them to play and to get the runners-up medals.

Then the coach congratulates Kez for volunteering to be goalie and thanks him for being brave.

Someone else on the team agrees and shouts "three cheers for Kez". And everyone cheers.

Hi Otto.

Otto's next door neighbour is Indra.

Otto thinks she must be quite old because she uses a stick to help her walk.

Indra cooks amazing samosas and brings them round to Otto's house.

Otto often sees rubbish in Indra's front garden.

Otto knows that the rubbish doesn't belong to Indra. He knows that other people have thrown it into Indra's garden.

Otto has seen Indra trying to tidy it up.

Indra struggles to do this as she needs one hand to hold her walking stick.

Otto knows it is time to use his superpower.
KINDNESS

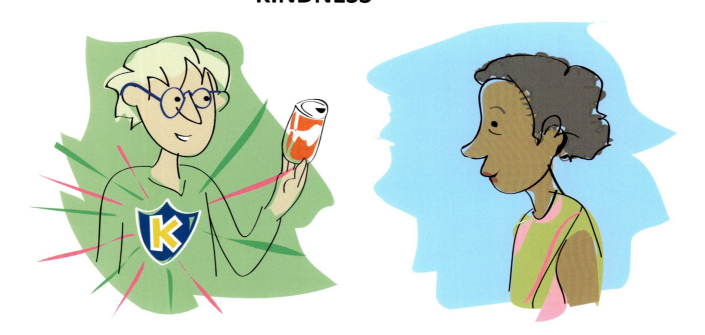

Otto goes round to Indra's house and offers to help her pick up the rubbish. Indra is really grateful.

Otto tells Indra she will not have to pick it up anymore as he will always do it for her and his friends will help too.

Otto, Coco, Ollie and Ling not only get samosas but gulab jamun too.

Hi Ollie.

Nina is new to Ollie's class. She has travelled from a country a long way away.

Ollie has seen how some of his classmates make fun of the way Nina speaks. She doesn't know many English words.

Someone sends Nina a mean message and someone else trips her over in the playground.

Ollie thought this was unkind.

Ollie knew it was time for his superpower.
KINDNESS

At lunchtime Ollie takes his tray to where Nina is sitting, on her own.

Ollie smiles at Nina and sits down next to her.

"Hi Nina. My name is Ollie. Welcome to our school."

After lunch Ollie takes Nina to meet some of his friends, Coco, Otto and Ling.

Hi Ling.

Ling loves dancing.

Every week she goes to her dance class.

Danny is the only boy in her class.

He loves dancing too.

Some of the girls in the dance class whisper about Danny.

Ling has seen them pull faces when Danny dances.

Danny has seen it too and says he doesn't want to come to class anymore.

Ling knows it is time for her superpower.
KINDNESS

Ling tells Danny she needs a partner for the class competition.

She asks Danny to be her partner and tells him she has lots of ideas for a dance they can do.

Danny has ideas too and they create their dance together.

Ling and Danny are the only girl and boy dancing together.

The judges are really pleased to see that their dance is so different to everyone else's.

Danny does some spins, Ling jumps and everyone claps at their dance routine.

Ling and Danny win the gold medal.

Coco, Otto and Ollie cheer
louder than anyone.

Coco, Otto, Ollie and Ling decide to do a presentation for their class.

Their presentation is called **'Cool to be Kind'**.

They want to help their classmates to see that they always have a choice to be kind.

They each talk about everyday acts of kindness.

And they talk about how they chose to be kind to Kez, Indra, Nina and Danny – when others were choosing to be unkind.

Coco suggests that every Monday morning, at the start of the day, the whole class close their eyes and think about what kind acts they could do for each other.

Otto suggests that every Friday afternoon, at the end of the day, the whole class close their eyes and think about what kind things they could do at home over the weekend.

Ollie suggests they make a kindness box for the class so that everyone can write down a kindness suggestion and put it in the box.

Ling suggests that everyone in the school should know about kindness, so she plans an assembly.

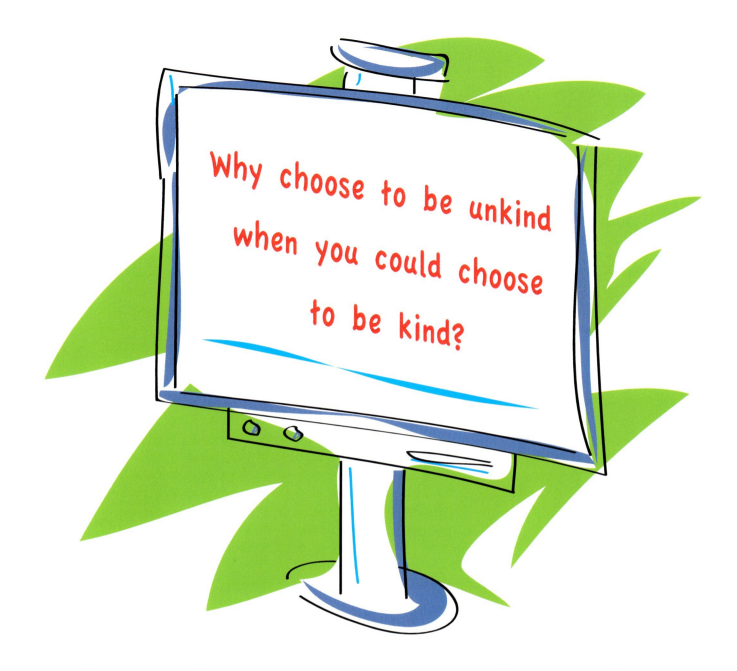

Their class teacher Ms Patterson suggests that the whole class learn about making kindness a choice.

She asks the class "Why choose to be unkind when you could choose to be kind?"

How can you be kind?